ADVE

South West Coast Path
South Cornwall

■ This new publication covers the South Cornwall section of the South West Coast Path, a National Trail extending 630 miles from Minehead in Somerset to Poole Harbour in Dorset and including a great variety of landscape, wildlife and geology.

■ Containing Ordnance Survey 'Explorer' maps in a convenient book format with an index to the main features, each of the five books show all footpaths, rights of way and public access land, and are the essential companion whether tackling the entire route or enjoying a relaxing afternoon walk in South Cornwall.

CONTENTS

Reference / Legend................2-3
Key to Map Pages...................4-7
Map Pages...........................8-57
Index...................................58-63
Route Planner......................64-65

Ferries...66
Tourist Information....................66
Safety & Security.......................67
QR codes..............................68-69

Geographers' A-Z Map Company Limited

Fairfield Road, Borough Green,
Sevenoaks, Kent TN15 8PP
Telephone: 01732 781000 (Enquiries & Trade Sales)
         01732 783422 (Retail Sales)
www.az.co.uk
Copyright © Geographers' A-Z Map Company Limited
EDITION 1   2013

Ordnance Survey

This product includes mapping data licensed from Ordnance Survey® with the permission of the Controller of Her Majesty's Stationery Office.

Mapping contents © Crown copyright and database rights 2012 Ordnance Survey 100017302

Communications

ROADS AND PATHS
Not necessarily rights of way

(S) Service Area	**7** Junction number

M 1 or A 6(M) — Motorway

A 35 — Dual carriageway

A 30 — Main road

B 3074 — Secondary road

— Narrow road with passing places

— Road under construction

— Road generally more than 4m wide

— Road generally less than 4m wide

— Other road, drive or track, fenced and unfenced

≫ — Gradient: steeper than 20% (1 in 5); 14% (1 in 7) to 20% (1 in 5)

Ferry — Ferry; Ferry P – passenger only

.... Path

RAILWAYS

— Multiple track standard gauge

— Single track standard gauge

—O— Narrow gauge or Light rapid transit system (LRTS) and station

— Road over; road under; level crossing

— Cutting; tunnel; embankment

—●— Station, open to passengers; siding

PUBLIC RIGHTS OF WAY

-------- Footpath   ———— Bridleway

+++++++ Byway open to all traffic

-+-+-+-+- Restricted byway (not for use by mechanically propelled vehicles)

Public rights of way shown on this map have been taken from local authority definitive maps and later amendments. Rights of way are liable to change and may not be clearly defined on the ground.
Please check with the relevant local authority for the latest information.

The representation on this map of any other road, track or path is no evidence of the existence of a right of way.

OTHER PUBLIC ACCESS

• • • Other routes with public access (not normally shown in urban areas)

The exact nature of the rights on these routes and the existence of any restrictions may be checked with the local highway authority. Alignments are based on the best information available.

  National Trail /

Long Distance Route

Recreational Route

--------- Permissive footpath

———— Permissive bridleway

Footpaths and bridleways along which landowners have permitted public use but which are not rights of way. The agreement may be withdrawn.

• • • Traffic-free cycle route

  National cycle network route number – traffic free

  National cycle network route number – on road

 DANGER AREA Firing and test ranges in the area. Danger! Observe warning notices

Visit www.access.mod.uk for information

ACCESS LAND

Portrayal of access land on this map is intended as a guide to land which is normally available for access on foot, for example access land created under the Countryside and Rights of Way Act 2000, and land managed by the National Trust, Forestry Commission and Woodland Trust. Access for other activities may also exist. Some restrictions will apply; some land will be excluded from open access rights.
The depiction of rights of access does not imply or express any warranty as to its accuracy or completeness. Observe local signs and follow the Countryside Code.

Visit www.countrysideaccess.gov.uk for up-to-date information

⬠ Access land boundary and tint

▢ Access land in woodland area

ℹ Access information point

 MANAGED ACCESS Access permitted within managed controls for example, local bylaws

Visit www.access.mod.uk for information

General Information

BOUNDARIES

— ·+· — ·+· — National

— · — · — · County (England)

— — — — Unitary Authority (UA), Metropolitan District (Met Dist), London Borough (LB) or District (Scotland & Wales are solely Unitary Authorities)

.... Civil Parish (CP) (England) or Community (C) (Wales)

—— National Park boundary

VEGETATION

Limits of vegetation are defined by positioning of symbols

  Coniferous trees

Non-coniferous trees

Coppice

Bracken, heath or rough grassland

  Orchard

Marsh, reeds or saltings

Scrub

GENERAL FEATURES

+	Place of worship	
	Current or former place of worship	
	with tower	
	with spire, minaret or dome	
	Building; important building	
	Glasshouse	
▲	Youth hostel	
■	Bunkhouse/camping barn/other hostel	
	Bus or coach station	
	Lighthouse; disused lighthouse; beacon	

△ Ⱶ	Triangulation pillar; mast
Ⱶ	Windmill, with or without sails
	Wind pump; wind turbine
pylon pole	Electricity transmission line
	Slopes
Gravel pit	Sand pit
Other pit or quarry	Landfill site or slag/spoil heap

BP/BS	Boundary post/stone
CG	Cattle grid
CH	Clubhouse
FB	Footbridge
MP ; MS	Milepost; milestone
Mon	Monument
PO	Post office
Pol Sta	Police station
Sch	School
TH	Town hall
NTL	Normal tidal limit
W; Spr	Well; spring

HEIGHTS AND NATURAL FEATURES

52 · Ground survey height
284 · Air survey height

Surface heights are to the nearest metre above mean sea level. Where two heights are shown, the first height is to the base of the triangulation pillar and the second (in brackets) to the highest natural point of the hill.

Vertical face/cliff

Loose rock   Boulders   Outcrop   Scree

Contours may be at 5 or 10 metres vertical interval

Water
Mud
Sand; sand & shingle

ARCHAEOLOGICAL AND HISTORICAL INFORMATION

	Site of antiquity	
⚔ 1066	Site of battle (with date)	
		* ⬚ Visible earthwork
		VILLA Roman
		Castle Non-Roman

Information provided by English Heritage for England and the Royal Commissions on the Ancient and Historical Monuments for Scotland and Wales

Selected Tourist and Leisure Information

P	Parking	
P&R	Park & Ride, - all year	
P&R	- seasonal	
i	Information cen. - all year	
i	- seasonal	
V	Visitor centre	
	Forestry Commission visitor centre	
	National Park Information cen.	
PC	Public convenience	
ℓ	Telephone - public	
ℓ	- roadside assistance	
ℓ	- emergency	

Ⱶ	Camp site
	Caravan site
	Recreation leisure sports centre
	Golf course or links
	Theme pleasure park
	Preserved railway
	Public house/s
	Craft centre
	Walks/trails
	Cycle trail
	Mountain bike trail

	Cycle hire
U	Horse riding
	Viewpoint
	Picnic site
	Country park
	Garden arboretum
	Water activities
	Slipway
	Boat trips
	Boat hire
	Nature reserve

	Fishing
☆	Other tourist feature
	Cathedral/Abbey
	Museum
	Castle/fort
	Building of historic interest
HC	Heritage centre
	National Trust
	English Heritage
	World Heritage site/area

1 Kilometre = 0.6214 mile
1 metre = 3.2808 feet

Scale 1:25 000

1 mile = 1.6093 kilometres
100 feet = 30.48 metres

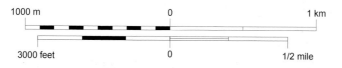

1000 m   0   1 km

3000 feet   0   1/2 mile

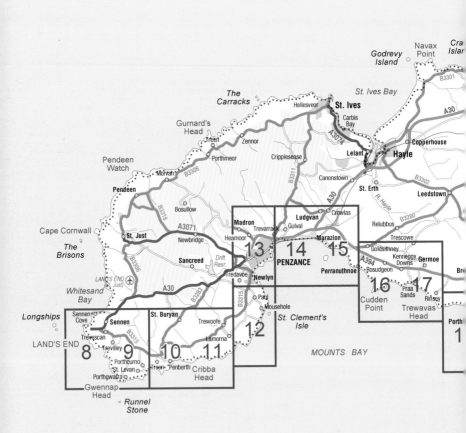

ATLANTIC *OCEAN*

Navax Point

Cra Islar

Godrevy Island

St. Ives Bay

B3301

A30

Hellesveor

St. Ives

Carbis Bay

Copperhouse

The Carracks

Lelant

Hayle

Gurnard's Head

Treen

Zennor

Cripplesease

A3074

B3302

Porthmeor

Canonstown

Leedstown

Pendeen Watch

Morvah

B3306

B3311

R. Hayle

St. Erth

Crowlas

B3280

Pendeen

Bosullow

B3318

A3071

Madron

Ludgvan

Relubbus

Trescowe

Cape Cornwall

Trevarrack

Gulval

Goldsithney

Kenneggy Downs

Germoe

The Brisons

St. Just

Newbridge

Heamoor

13

14

Marazion

15

A394

Bosudgeon

Br

Sancreed

Drift Resr.

PENZANCE

16

17

Whitesand Bay

B3006

A30

B3283

Tredavoe

Perranuthnoe

Praa Sands

Rinsey

Longships

LAND'S END (J. Just)

Newlyn

B3315

Paul

Cudden Point

Trewavas Head

Porth

1

LAND'S END

Sennen Cove

Sennen

St. Buryan

Trewoofe

Mousehole

St. Clement's Isle

8

B3315

Trevescan

Trevilley

9

10

11

12

MOUNTS BAY

Porthcurno

St. Levan

Treen

Penberth

Lamorna

Porthgwarra

Gwennap Head

Cribba Head

Runnel Stone

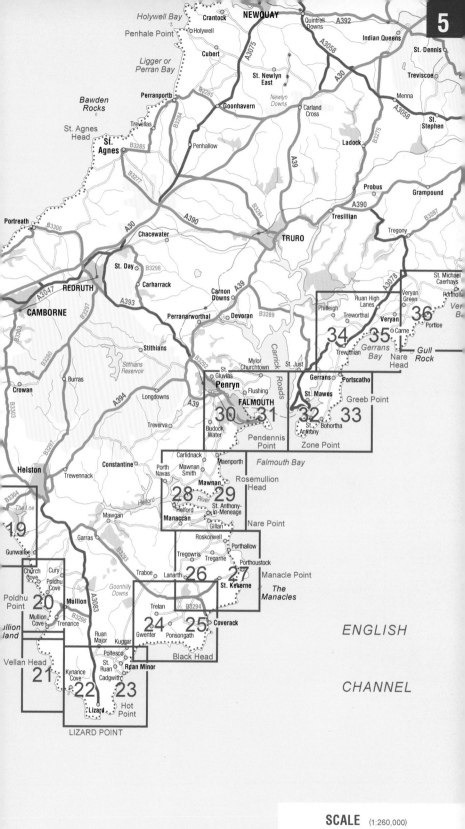

NEWQUAY

Holywell Bay
Crantock
Penhale Point
Quintrell Downs
A392
A3075
Holywell
A3058
Indian Queens
St. Dennis
Cubert
Ligger or Perran Bay
St. Newlyn East
Newlyn Downs
A30
Treviscoe
Menna
St. Stephen
A3058
Perranporth
Goonhavern
Carland Cross
B3285
Bawden Rocks
Trevellas
Penhallow
B3284
Ladock
B3275
Probus
Grampound
St. Agnes Head
St. Agnes
B3285
A39
B3287
B3277
Tresillian
A390
Tregony
Portreath
B3300
Chacewater
TRURO
B3078
St. Michael Caerhays
Portholl
Veryan Green
Ver Ba
St. Day
B3298
Carnon Downs
A39
Philleigh
Ruan High Lanes
Veryan
Carne
Portloe
REDRUTH
A3047
A393
Carharrack
36
34
35
Gerrans Bay
Nare Head
Gull Rock
CAMBORNE
B3297
Perranarworthal
Devoran
B3289
Trewithian
Trewortha
St. Just
B3303
Stithians
B3292
St. Gluvias
Penryn
Mylor Churchtown
Gerrans
Portscatho
Greeb Point
Crowan
Burras
Longdowns
Flushing
St. Mawes
B3280
A394
Treverva
A39
FALMOUTH
32
33
B3003
Helston
Trewennack
Constantine
A394
30
31
St. Anthony
Bohortha
Zone Point
Pendennis Point
Treverva
Budock Water
Carlidnack
Maenporth
Falmouth Bay
B3304
The Loe
Mawgan
Porth Navas
Mawnan Smith
Rosemullion Head
19
Gunwalloe
Helford
Mawnan
St. Anthony-in-Meneage
Nare Point
28
29
River
Church Cove
Cury
Poldhu Cove
Manaccan
Gillan
Roskorwell
Porthallow
Poldhu Point
20
Mullion
Garras
Tregowris
Tregarne
Porthoustock
Mullion Cove
B3296
Trenance
A3083
Traboe
Lanarth
26
27
Manacle Point
B3263
Goonhilly Downs
St. Keverne
The Manacles
ullion land
Ruan Major
Kuggar
Trelan
B3294
Vellan Head
21
Kynance Cove
St. Ruan
Poltesco
24
25
Coverack
22
23
Cadgwith
Gwenter
Ponsongath
Black Head
Ruan Minor
Lizard
Hot Point
LIZARD POINT

ENGLISH

CHANNEL

KEY TO MAP PAGES

Trevone
Rock
Padstow
Bodieve
St. Issey
A389
Wadebridge
St. Mabyn
B3314
St. Tudy
R. Allen
A39
St. Breward
De Lank River
Garrow Tor
Blisland
A30
Colliford Lake
B3276
St. Breock Downs
R. Camel
Washaway
A389
Bodmin
Cardinham
St. Neot
A38
St. Mawgan
NEWQUAY CORNWALL
Vale of Mawgan
St. Wenn
Withiel
Lanivet
A30
Maudlin
R. Fowey
Middle Taphouse
A390
B3359
Port Resr.
A3059
St. Columb Major
A392
Roche
Lanlivery
Lostwithiel
Indian Queens
B3274
Bugle
Luxulyan
A390
Golant
Lanreath
Pe
A30
B3279
St. Dennis
Hensbarrow Downs
Stenalees
A391
St. Blazey
Treviscoe
Nanpean
Foxhole
St. Blazey Gate
Tregrehan Mills
Par
Tywardreath
Lanteglos Highway
Penpoll
Trenewan
Menna
A3058
Trewoon
ST. AUSTELL
Boscoppa
Holmbush
Polkerris
Fowey
Bodinnick
Lansallos
4
Ladock
B3275
St. Stephen
Charlestown
42
Carlyon Bay
43
Menabilly
44
45
Polruan
46
A390
Higher Porthpean
St. Austell Bay
Gribbin Head
Pencarrow Head
Probus
Grampound
B3287
Polgooth
Trenarren
Black Head
35mins. (Seasonal)
Tresillian
St. Ewe
40
Pentewan
41
Tregony
Kestle
Treniskey
Mevagissey Bay
A3078
Portmellon
Mevagissey
Trevarrick
Gorran High Lanes
Chapel Point
St. Michael Caerhays
Rescassa
Gorran Churchtown
Gorran Haven
Ruan High Lanes
Veryan Green
Porthholland
Boswinger
38
39
Treworthal
Veryan
36
Portloe
37
Veryan Bay
Pengare
Dodman Point
35
Carne
Gull Rock
Gerrans Bay
Nare Head
Portscatho
Greeb Point
33
Bohortha
Point

ENGLISH

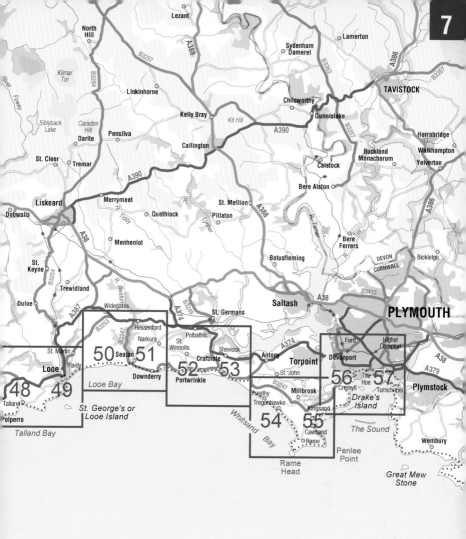

Lezant

North Hill

Lamerton

Sydenham Damerel

Kilmar Tor

Linkinhorne

Kelly Bray

Chilsworthy

Gunnislake

TAVISTOCK

Siblyback Lake

Caradon Hill

Pensilva

Darite

Callington

Kit Hill

A390

Calstock

Horrabridge

Walkhampton

Yelverton

St. Cleer

Tremar

Liskeard

Merrymeet

Quethiock

Pillaton

St. Mellion

Bere Alston

Botusfleming

Bere Ferrers

DEVON

CORNWALL

Bickleigh

Dobwalls

Menheniot

Trewidland

Duloe

St. Keyne

Widegates

Hessenford

Narkurs

St. Germans

Saltash

PLYMOUTH

St. Martin

Looe

Plaidy

50 Seaton **51**

Downderry

Polbathic

St. Winnolls

Crafthole

Sheviock

Antony

Torpoint

Ford

Higher Compton

Devonport

56 **57**

The Hoe

Cremyll

Turnchapel

Plymstock

48 **49**

Talland

Looe Bay

52 Portwrinkle **53**

St. John

Millbrook

Drake's Island

Polperro

St. George's or Looe Island

Freathy

Tregonhawke

54

Kingsand

55

Cawsand

Rame

The Sound

Wembury

Talland Bay

Whitsand Bay

Penlee Point

Rame Head

Great Mew Stone

Eddystone Rocks

CHANNEL

Land's End

Pedn-mên-du
Irish Lady
Castle Zawn
Gamper
Dr Syntax's Head
The Peal
Peber
Dr Johnson's Head
Carn Kez
Greeb Zawn
Armed Knight
Enys Dodnan
Zawn Wells
Pordenack Point
Lion's Den
Zawn Trevilley
Carn Boel
Carn Les Boel

The Tribbens
Jetty
Sennen Cove
Cumulus Cairn
Mayon Cliff
Maen Castle Fort
Carn Clog
Trevescan Cliff
Legendary Land's End
Hotel
Carn Greeb
Carn Cheer
South West Coast Path
Trevilley Cliff
Zawn Reeth
Carn Cravah
Cave
Bosistow
Mill Bay or Nanjizal
Fort
Bosistow Island
Pendower Co
Zawn Kelly
Black
Carn

Rectory
Standing Stone
Treve Common
Spring
Trevescan
Trev
Cross
Cross

MHW
MLW

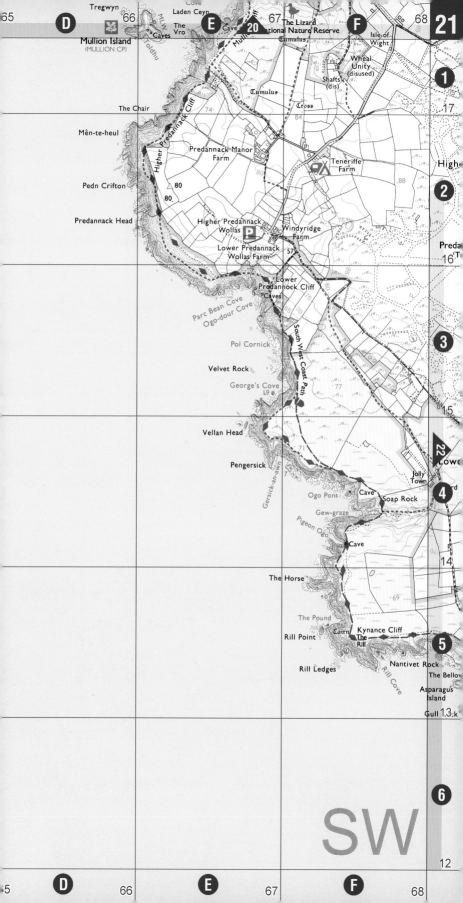

Tresaddern

Tesco Valley 72

Kuggar

1

Corgerrick

Caerverracks

16

Trowgey Farm

FB

Treal

Crig-a-tana Rocks

Mean Low Water

Thorny Cliff

Tumuli

36

60

Polstangey Bridge

Polbream Point

Treveddon

Little Cove

Carleon Cove

Poltesco

Poltesco Rock

2

Treleague Farm

68

White House Farm

Carleon Cottage

Black Rock

64

48

St Ruan

P

Sch

FB

PO

Treworder

Ruan Minor

65

°15

FBs

W

Barn Hill

Enys Head

Kildown Cove

Brandise

Bruggan Farm

St Ruan's Well

P

PO

60

50

Kildown Point

3

Cadgwith

29

9

Terrick Colt

Cadgwith Cove

Little Cove

Prazegooth

W

14

Grade

76

Gwavas Vean

Devil's Frying Pan

Gwavas Farm

Carn Barrow

Dollar Ogo

Caves

Caves

Chough's Ogo

Polgwidden

4

Polbarrow

Whale Rock

The Chair

63

Parn Voose Cove

13

Quarry (dis)

The Balk

Church Cove

ch

Kilcobben Cove

Lifeboat Station

Green Lane

62

Prilla Cove

5

rds Road

Hot Point

Spr

69

Pyg

12

Bass Point

Lookout Station

Bay

Pen Olver

6

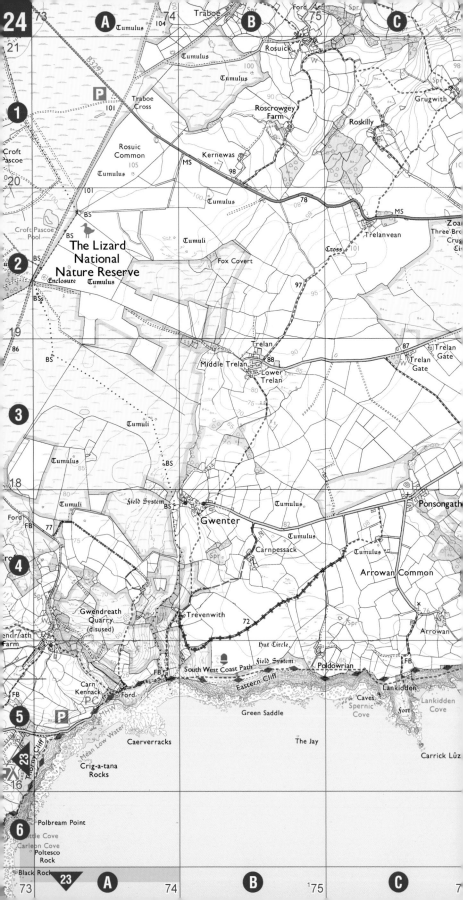

Farm

P PC

Maenporth
Estate

Maenporth

1

MHW

Settlement

FB

High Cliff
Caves

44

FB

Hotel
Meudon

The Hutches

Mawnan
Smith

2

Hotel

Bream Cove

Chenhalls

Treworgan

arwinion

Hotel
64

Spr

Gatamala Cove

Nansidwell
Farm

Rosemullion
Head

67

Rosemullion

South West Coast Path

73

Trerose

Prisk Cove

3

Mawnan

P

Trerose
House

August
Rock

3

Shag Rock

ack

Parson's Beach

Toll Point

Mawnan Shear

4

The Gew

Tendera
S P
hony-
neage

Spr

Dennis
Head

Little
Dennis

Gillan
Harbour

The Crook

5

Mên-aver Point

Spr

Nare Point

Gillan

Mên-aver Beach

Observation Post (MOD)
Lookout Station

Parbean
Cove

Lestowder Cliff

Polnare Cove

SW

Tregasso

Spr

Lestowder

33

Nare Head

6

GE

Spr

Trewarnevas

Pennare
House

Pennare
Barton

Bass Rock
PC Portscatho
The Porth
Pencabe
rrans
s Bay
el
64
Sch
60
Treloan
Spr
arton
rane
28
Spr
Long Drang

Raven's Hole

South West Coast Path

46

37
The Lodge
Rosteague
MHW
MLW
Greeb Point

Towan Beach

Island Rock
Killigerran
Head

hmellin
Head

1
2
3
4
5
6

⁰35
34
33
32
31
⁰30

SW

Folkirft Beach

Portmellon Cove

44

Portmellon

1

Bodrugan
Barton

Roward's Quay

Chapel Point

Colona Beach

Old Walls

Turbot Point

43

Earthwork

Tumulus

South West Coast Path

Pabyer Point

Carn
Rocks

2

ewollock

Jobbles Rock

Great Perhaver
Beach

Gwineas or Gwinges

42

Great Perhaver
Point

3

Little Perhaver
Point

PO

PC

Pen-a-maen or
Maenease Point

Little Sand Cove

41

Cadythew Rock

r Vault
each

4

⁰40

5

39

SX

6

Lobb's Shop
Reservoir
107

FB

Gwendra Point

Ropehaven Cliffs
Nature Reserve

1

49

P

ST AUSTELL
BAY CP

CP

Trevissick
Sprs

Ropehaven

Ledrah
Trenarren
84

Gerrans Point

2

Hydraulic Ram

75

Iglaze

70

Hallane

The Bite

Sprs

The Vans

65

Porthtowan

60

Rifle Range

48

Adit
Quarries
(dis)

South West Coast Path

Drennick

Fort

Black Head

Quarry
(dis)

3

Polrudden
Farm

Polrudden Cove

Point of Well

47

Pentewan

Gamas Point

Pentewan
Beach

4

Low Water

46

Penare Point

Mevagissey Bay

5

45

FERRY
SHIP
Fowey (P) (Summer)

Point

6

SX

44

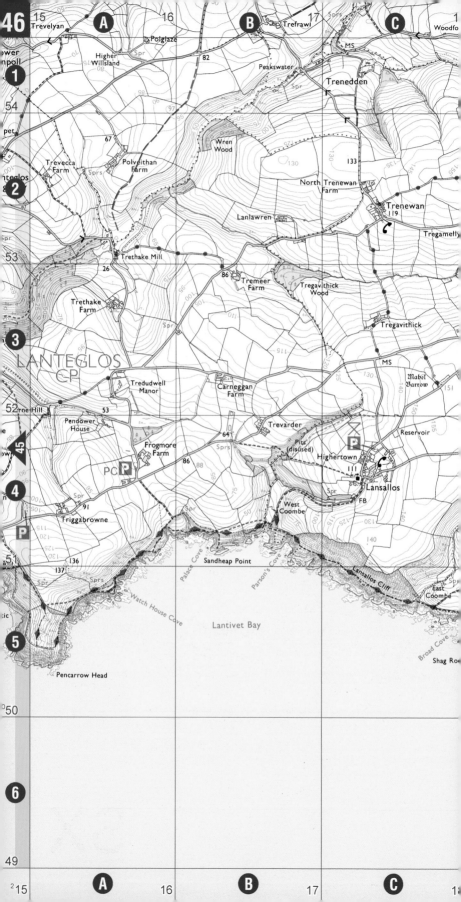

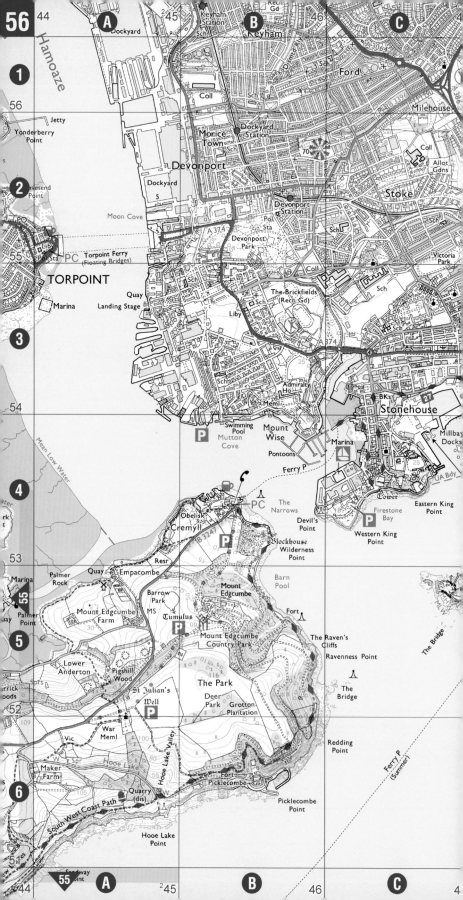

FERRIES
SHIP
Roscoff (Summer)
Santander (Summer)

PLYMOUTH

The Sound

Drake's or St Nicholas's
Island
(CITY OF PLYMOUTH)

HOW TO USE THIS INDEX

1. The map reference given refers to the actual square in which the feature is located and not the name.

2. A strict alphabetical order is used e.g. Porthcurnick Beach follows Porth Chapel but precedes Porth Curno

3. Names prefixed with 'The' are indexed under the main name, for example 'The Beacon' appears as 'Beacon, The'

THE NATIONAL GRID REFERENCING SYSTEM

The grid lines form part of the National Grid and are at 1 km intervals.

To give a unique reference position of a point to within 100 metres proceed as follows:

Sample point: **Anderton**

1. Read letters identifying 100,000 metre square in which the point lies (**SX**)

2. FIRST QUOTE EASTINGS - locate the first VERTICAL grid line to LEFT of the point and read the BLUE figures labelling the line in the top or bottom margin of the page (**42**). Estimate tenths from the grid line to the point (**5**). This gives a figure of **425**

3. THEN QUOTE NORTHINGS - locate the first HORIZONTAL grid line BELOW the point and read the BLUE figures labelling the line in the left or right margin of the page (**51**). Estimate tenths from the grid line to the point (**2**). This gives a figure of **512**

Sample Reference: **Anderton SX 425 512**

Name	Ref	Grid
Amsterdam Point	.4B 32	SW 851 325
Anderton	.3D 55	SX 425 512
Angrouse Cliff	.4B 20	SW 664 193
Appletree Point	.4B 42	SX 043 515
Ardensawah Cliff	.5D 9	SW 360 227
Arrowan Common	.4C 24	SW 753 172
Ashton	.3F 17	SW 601 285
Badger's Cross	.1A 14	SW 485 331
Balwest	.2F 17	SW 595 299
Barbican	.3E 57	SX 481 541
Barcelona	.3B 48	SX 220 535
Barn Pool	.5B 56	SX 456 528
Basore Point	.5F 15	SW 531 294
Bass Point	.6D 23	SW 716 118
Battern Cliffs	.4F 51	SX 329 541
Baulk Head	.6F 19	SW 654 221
Beacon, The	.3C 52	SX 351 543
Beagles Hole	.5D 25	SW 768 163
Beagles Point	.5D 25	SW 766 165
Berepper	.6F 19	SW 658 229
Berry Down	.2E 53	SX 375 553
Bessy's Cove	.4B 16	SW 557 278
Bethel	.3A 42	SX 034 529
Biscovey	.2D 43	SX 064 532
Bissom	.2B 30	SW 792 349
Black Carn	.5D 9	SW 360 222
Black Head	.3E 41	SX 039 478
	.5E 25	SW 778 161
Blackybale Point	.5D 47	SX 187 502
Blarrick Cliff	.4F 53	SX 381 530
Blouth Point	.6A 36	SW 928 379
Bodigga Cliff	.4A 50	SX 273 542
Bodinnick	.3E 45	SX 130 521
Bodinnick Car Park	.3D 45	SX 129 524
Bodinnick Ferry	.3D 45	SX 127 522
Bohortha	.4C 32	SW 861 322
Bosahan Cove	.4C 28	SW 773 263
Boscawen Cliff	.5E 11	SW 432 229
Boscawen Point	.5E 11	SW 431 228
Boscoppa	.2A 42	SX 033 536
Boscreege	.1F 17	SW 590 302
Boskenna Cliff	.4D 11	SW 425 231
Boslowick	.5B 30	SW 795 314
Bosveal Car Park	.3C 28	SW 774 277
Boswinger	.3B 38	SW 991 412
Boswinger Youth Hostel	.3B 38	SW 990 410
Bottoms	.3F 9	SW 385 242
Bow Beach	.4C 38	SX 008 407
Bream Cove	.2E 29	SW 791 285
Brent	.5A 48	SX 213 512
Britain Point	.4C 52	SX 350 538
Broad Cove	.5C 46	SX 179 506
Budock Water	.4A 30	SW 783 323
Bull Cove	.6D 55	SX 421 484
Bullion Cliff	.2C 18	SW 620 262
Butter Cove	.5D 25	SW 761 166
Cadgwith	.3E 23	SW 721 145
Cadgwith Car Park	.3D 23	SW 719 147
Cadgwith Cove	.3E 23	SW 722 1
Caerhays Castle	.2F 37	SW 970 4
Caerthillian Cove	.5B 22	SW 694 1
Captain Blake's Point	.5C 54	SX 419 4
Caragloose Point	.4C 36	SW 946 3
Carey Park	.5A 48	SX 214 5
Cargloth Cliffs	.4A 52	SX 337 5
Carleon Cove	.2E 23	SW 728 1
Carlthey Point	.5B 38	SW 997 3
Carlyon Bay	.3C 42	SX 056 5
Carminowe Creek	.4E 19	SW 649 2
Carn Barges	.4F 11	SW 446 2
Carn Boel	.4B 8	SW 348 2
Carn-du	.5A 12	SW 457 2
Carne	.3F 35	SW 913 3
Carne Beach	.3E 35	SW 905 3
Carne Beach Car Park	.3E 35	SW 906 3
Carne Beacon	.3F 35	SW 912 3
Carn Guthensbrås	.6D 9	SW 362 2
Carn Kez	.3B 8	SW 341 2
Carn Mellyn	.5A 12	SW 450 2
Carn Scathe	.6E 9	SW 372 2
Carn Towan	.1D 9	SW 361 2
Carracawn Cross	.1F 51	SX 321 5
Carrag-a-pilaz Car Park	.3B 20	SW 662 2
Carricknath Point	.5A 32	SW 845 3
Carrickowel Point	.5A 42	SX 034 5
Carrick Roads	.2F 31	SW 834 3
Carwinion Gardens	.2D 29	SW 782 2
Castle Point	.4A 32	SW 840 3
Castle Zawn	.2B 8	SW 347 2
Cattedown	.4F 57	SX 493 5
Cattewater	.4F 57	SX 491 5
Cawsand	.4E 55	SX 434 5
Cawsand Bay	.4F 55	SX 441 5
Cawsand Car Park	.4E 55	SX 431 5
Cellars Beach	.4B 32	SW 852 3
Chapel Cliff	.5F 47	SX 209 5
Chapel Point	.1E 39	SX 028 4
Charlestown	.4A 42	SX 037 5
Charlestown Car Park	.4A 42	SX 037 5
Charlestown Shipwreck & Heritage Centre	.4A 42	SX 039 5
Chough's Ogo	.4E 23	SW 720 1
Church Cove	.5D 23	SW 711 1
	.5D 23	SW 714 1
Church Cove (Gunwalloe)	.3B 20	SW 661 2
Chyandour	.3F 13	SW 479 3
Chyanvounder	.6F 19	SW 657 2
Chynhalls Cliff	.4F 25	SW 781 1
Chynhalls Point	.4F 25	SW 786 1
Chyvarloe	.5F 19	SW 653 2
Chyvarloe (Loe Bar East) Car Park	.5F 19	SW 652 2
Cobland Hill	.3B 52	SX 342 5
Colona Beach	.1E 39	SX 026 4
Colors Cove	.5D 47	SX 189 5
Compton	.1F 57	SX 495 5
Coombe Farm Car Park	.4B 44	SX 109 5
Coombe Haven	.5C 44	SX 113 5
Coverack	.3F 25	SW 782 1
Coverack Car Park	.3F 25	SW 781 1

Name	Grid Ref 1	Grid Ref 2
...verack Youth Hostel	3F 25	SW 782 181
...afthole	3D 53	SX 366 541
...ane Cove	5C 54	SX 418 491
...eek Stephen Point	4C 34	SW 886 371
...emyll	4B 56	SX 453 533
...emyll Car Park	4B 56	SX 452 533
...emyll Ferry	4B 56	SX 457 536
...bba Head	5B 10	SW 403 224
...ipp's Cove	5A 10	SW 398 220
...oft Pascoe Pool	2A 24	SW 731 197
...ousa Downs	3D 25	SW 761 189
...owlas	1D 15	SW 515 331
...umplehorn	4F 47	SX 205 514
...umplehorn Car Park	4F 47	SX 206 516
...dden Point	4A 16	SW 548 275
...rgurrell	4C 34	SW 883 374
...ry	2C 20	SW 678 213
...an Point	5E 27	SW 805 204
...gibna Chapel (Loe Pool East) Car Park	3F 19	SW 653 251
...nnis Head	5D 29	SW 788 256
...evil's Frying Pan	3E 23	SW 720 142
...evonport	2B 56	SX 451 556
...evonport Station	2B 56	SX 457 554
...nas Cove	5E 25	SW 774 162
...ockyard Station	2B 56	SX 453 558
... Johnson's Head	2B 8	SW 341 250
... Syntax's Head	2B 8	SW 341 253
...odman Point	5C 38	SX 001 391
...ollar Ogo	4E 23	SW 720 139
...olor Point	3F 25	SW 785 181
...ownas Cove	5D 25	SW 764 167
...ownderry	4E 51	SX 317 540
...ownderry Beach	5E 51	SX 316 538
...ownderry, Broads Yard Car Park	4E 51	SX 314 540
...ownend Point	6B 48	SX 220 508
...rake's Island	5C 56	SX 468 528
...unker Point	5E 49	SX 255 514
...uporth	4A 42	SX 033 513
...urgan	3C 28	SW 773 273
...stern King Point	4C 56	SX 466 534
...st Looe	3E 49	SX 256 532
...st Portholland	2E 37	SW 960 412
...len Project	1B 42	SX 048 546
...larooze Cliff	4B 52	SX 345 539
...winick Cove	4C 32	SW 867 320
...ays Head	3E 23	SW 728 149
...th Hill	1F 53	SX 380 560
...lmouth	4C 30	SW 809 326
...lmouth Bay	6D 31	SW 812 302
...lmouth Docks Station	4D 31	SW 817 323
...lmouth, Gyllyngvase Beach Car Park	5C 30	SW 807 317
...lmouth Lifeboat Station	4D 31	SW 814 324
...lmouth, Maritime Museum Car Park		
	4D 31	SW 813 322
...lmouth Park & Ride	3B 30	SW 795 338
...lmouth, Pendennis Castle Car Park	4E 31	SW 823 320
...lmouth, Pendennis Pavilion Car Park		
	4E 31	SW 821 321
...lmouth, Pendennis Point Car Park	5E 31	SW 826 315
...lmouth Tourist Information Centre	4C 30	SW 807 329
...lmouth, Town Quarry (Quarry Hill) Car Park		
	4C 30	SW 804 328
...lmouth Town Station	4D 31	SW 810 320
...l-Ruan Estuary Nature Reserve	1B 34	SW 874 406
...nnypool Beach	4C 52	SX 359 537
...shing Point	3D 43	SX 067 521
...etching's Cove	2D 27	SW 797 237
...ushing	3C 30	SW 808 339
...olly Cove	5D 9	SW 360 223
...rd	1C 56	SX 462 562
...owey	4D 45	SX 125 516
...owey, Albert Quay Car Park	4D 45	SX 126 518
...owey, Caffa Mill Car Park	3D 45	SX 126 522
...owey Lifeboat Station	3D 45	SX 128 520
...owey, Main Car Park	4D 45	SX 122 516
...owey Museum	4D 45	SX 126 516
...owey, Readymoney Car Park	4C 44	SX 116 513
...owey Tourist Information Centre	4D 45	SX 125 516
...eathy	2A 54	SX 398 520
...eathy Car Park	2A 54	SX 394 523
...eathy Cliff	3A 54	SX 397 519
...ogmore Car Park	4A 46	SX 157 516
Gamas Point	3D 41	SX 023 471
Gamper	2B 8	SW 344 256
	5B 10	SW 402 220
Gatamala Cove	2E 29	SW 793 282
Gell Point	5B 38	SW 994 398
George's Cove	3E 21	SW 669 151
Germoe	2E 17	SW 585 293
Germoe Cross Roads	2E 17	SW 582 291
Gerrans	1D 33	SW 871 351
Gerrans Bay	4E 35	SW 901 371
Gerrans Car Park	1D 33	SW 872 350
Gerrans Point	2E 41	SX 039 487
Gew-graze	4F 21	SW 674 143
Giant's Quoits	4E 27	SW 804 214
Gillan	5D 29	SW 785 251
Gillan Creek	5C 28	SW 776 251
Gillan Creek Ferry	5D 29	SW 780 253
Gillan Harbour	5D 29	SW 782 255
Glendurgan Garden	3C 28	SW 772 277
Godrevy Cove	5E 27	SW 806 208
Golant	1D 45	SX 122 546
Goldsithney	1A 16	SW 545 306
Gorran Churchtown	2B 38	SW 999 422
Gorran Haven	3D 39	SX 012 415
Gorran Haven Car Park	3D 39	SX 010 415
Gorran High Lanes	1A 38	SW 988 431
Great Lantic Beach	5F 45	SX 147 508
Great Perhaver Beach	2D 39	SX 016 422
Great Perhaver Point	3D 39	SX 014 419
Greeb Point	4A 38	SW 982 405
	3D 33	SW 877 336
Gribbin Daymark (Tower)	6A 44	SX 097 497
Gribbin Head	6A 44	SX 096 494
Gull Rock	6A 36	SW 927 368
Gulval	3A 14	SW 484 317
Gunwalloe	6F 19	SW 656 227
Gunwalloe Church Cove Car Park	3A 20	SW 659 208
Gunwalloe Fishing Cove	6F 19	SW 654 223
Gwallon	3E 15	SW 525 319
Gwavas Lake	6F 13	SW 476 284
Gwendra Point	1E 41	SX 033 493
Gwennap Head	6D 9	SW 367 214
Gwenter	4B 24	SW 741 178
Gyllyngvase Beach	5C 30	SW 809 316
Halamanning	1C 16	SW 561 309
Halzephron Cove	2A 20	SW 655 217
Hamoaze	1A 56	SX 440 563
Hannafore	4E 49	SX 256 525
Hannafore Beach	4E 49	SX 256 524
Hannafore Point	4E 49	SX 258 523
Hard Head	5F 47	SX 201 507
Hartriza Point	4C 36	SW 942 396
Heamoor	3E 13	SW 463 311
Helford	4A 28	SW 757 260
Helford Car Park	4A 28	SW 759 261
Helford Ferry	4B 28	SW 761 266
Helford Passage	4B 28	SW 763 269
Helford Point	4B 28	SW 760 264
Helford River	4B 28	SW 763 266
Helston	1F 19	SW 660 274
Helston, Castle Green Car Park	1F 19	SW 656 273
Helston, Fairground Car Park	2F 19	SW 653 269
Helston Tourist Information Centre	1F 19	SW 659 273
Hemmick Beach	4B 38	SW 994 404
Hendersick Car Park	4C 48	SX 236 520
Hendra	4F 17	SW 591 278
Hessenford	1D 51	SX 307 574
Higher Bosistow Cliff	4C 8	SW 358 233
Higher Downs	1B 16	SW 551 309
Higher Kenneggy	3C 16	SW 560 287
Higher Porthpean	5A 42	SX 029 504
Higher Predannack Cliff	2E 21	SW 661 168
Higher Predannack Downs	1A 22	SW 683 166
High Point	5B 38	SW 996 396
Holmbush	3A 42	SX 035 526
Holseer Cove	5B 22	SW 694 121
Homebarton Hill	6D 55	SX 429 489
Hooe Lake Point	6A 56	SX 448 513
Hot Point	5D 23	SW 717 122
Housel Bay	6C 22	SW 709 115
Housel Cove	6C 22	SW 708 119
Inner Broady Cove	5F 55	SX 442 491
Inner Penlee Point	5F 55	SX 442 492

Insworke	2E 55	SX 430 527
Inswork Point	1E 55	SX 438 533
Jacka Point	4B 36	SW 938 392
Jennycliff Bay	5E 57	SX 488 520
Jennycliff Bay Car Park	5F 57	SX 492 523
Kemyel Cliff	4A 12	SW 457 241
Kemyel Crease Nature Reserve	4A 12	SW 459 244
Kemyel Point	4B 12	SW 460 240
Kennack Sands Car Park	1F 23	SW 732 164
Kenneggy Cliff	3C 16	SW 562 283
Kenneggy Downs	2C 16	SW 568 291
Kenneggy Sand	3C 16	SW 561 281
Kerslake Cliff	4E 53	SX 375 533
Kestle	5A 40	SW 990 453
Keveral Beach	4C 50	SX 293 542
Keyham Station	1B 56	SX 451 567
Kiberick Cove	6A 36	SW 925 379
Kilcobben Cove	5D 23	SW 715 125
Kildown Cove	3E 23	SW 727 148
Kildown Point	3E 23	SW 726 146
Killigerran Head	4D 33	SW 870 322
Kilminorth Woods Nature Reserve	2D 49	SX 242 542
Kingsand	4E 55	SX 434 505
King's Cove	4B 16	SW 558 278
King's Wood Car Park	2B 40	SX 006 488
Kuggar	1E 23	SW 724 163
Kynance Cliff	5F 21	SW 675 135
Kynance Cove	4A 22	SW 684 132
Kynance Cove Car Park	4A 22	SW 688 132
Lady Cove	6E 55	SX 439 487
Laira	2F 57	SX 500 553
Laira Bridge	3F 57	SX 501 542
Lambsowden Cove	4A 38	SW 982 406
Lamledra (Vault Beach) Car Park	3D 39	SX 011 410
Lamorna	3F 11	SW 445 245
Lamorna Cove	5A 12	SW 452 238
Lamorna Cove Car Park	3F 11	SW 449 240
Lamorna Point	5A 12	SW 450 236
Lamorran House Gardens	3A 32	SW 843 331
Lancrion Point	4B 42	SX 046 515
Land's End	2B 8	SW 342 250
Land's End Car Park	2B 8	SW 344 250
Lankelly Cliff	5B 44	SX 105 503
Lankidden Cove	5C 24	SW 756 166
Lansallos	4C 46	SX 173 515
Lansallos Car Park	4C 46	SX 173 517
Lansallos Cliff	5C 46	SX 173 509
Lanteglos Highway	2F 45	SX 147 536
Lantic Bay	5F 45	SX 143 506
Lantivet Bay	5B 46	SX 163 506
Leggan Cove	4E 27	SW 807 211
Le Scathe Cove	5B 10	SW 406 227
Levalsa Meor	1B 40	SX 005 492
Lillery's Cove	6D 55	SX 424 486
Little Cove	2E 23	SW 728 157
	3E 23	SW 722 143
Little Lantic Beach	5F 45	SX 148 506
Little Perhaver Point	3D 39	SX 013 416
Little Sand Cove	3D 39	SX 016 411
Lizard	5C 22	SW 706 125
Lizard Downs	4B 22	SW 694 139
Lizard Lighthouse	6C 22	SW 704 116
Lizard National Nature Reserve, The	4A 22	SW 689 138
	2A 24	SW 733 197
Lizard Point	6B 22	SW 694 115
Lizard Point Car Park	6C 22	SW 702 116
Lizard Point Youth Hostel	6C 22	SW 703 115
Lizard Pool	5B 38	SW 999 392
Loe, The	3E 19	SW 647 250
Loe Bar	4E 19	SW 643 241
Logan Rock	6A 10	SW 396 219
Long Cove	5C 54	SX 417 490
Long Point	2E 37	SW 969 410
Longrock	3B 14	SW 499 313
Long Rock Car Park	3B 14	SW 496 312
Long Sands	4E 53	SX 376 531
Looe	3E 49	SX 254 536
Looe Bay	4F 49	SX 264 529
Looe Island	5E 49	SX 258 514
Looe Island Nature Reserve	5E 49	SX 257 513
Looe Lifeboat Station	3E 49	SX 256 531
Looe, Millpool Car Park	3E 49	SX 251 537
Looe Station	3E 49	SX 253 5
Looe Tourist Information Centre	3E 49	SX 254 5
Lost Gardens of Heligan	4A 40	SW 997 4
Lower Bosistow Cliff	4C 8	SW 357 2
Lower Porthpean	5A 42	SX 030 5
Lower Predannack Downs	3A 22	SW 683 1
Lowland Point	6E 27	SW 803 1
Ludgvan	1C 14	SW 504 3
Madron	3D 13	SW 453 3
Maen Castle	2B 8	SW 347 2
Maen-du Point	5F 15	SW 535 2
Maenease Point	3D 39	SX 017 4
Maenporth	1D 29	SW 789 2
Maenporth Car Park	1D 29	SW 789 2
Malmanare Point	4F 35	SW 915 3
Manaccan	5B 28	SW 763 2
Manacle Point	4F 27	SW 811 2
Manacles, The	5F 27	SW 818 2
Mannamead	1E 57	SX 487 5
Marazion	4D 15	SW 518 3
Marazion, Charity Car Park	3D 15	SW 512 3
Marazion Marsh Nature Reserve	3D 15	SW 510 3
Marazion Museum	4D 15	SW 518 3
Marazion, Station Car Park	3C 14	SW 506 3
Marconi Monument	4B 20	SW 663 1
Marsh Villa Gardens	1E 43	SX 077 5
Mawnan	3D 29	SW 787 2
Mawnan Church Car Park	3D 29	SW 787 2
Mawnan Smith	2C 28	SW 778 2
Mayon	2C 8	SW 358 2
Mayon Cliff	2B 8	SW 348 2
Melinsey Mill Museum	2E 35	SW 905 3
Menabilly Car Park	4A 44	SX 096 5
Menare Point	5B 36	SW 934 3
Merry Maidens Stone Circle	3E 11	SW 432 2
Merthen Point	5C 10	SW 418 2
Mevagissey	6C 40	SX 014 4
Mevagissey Bay	5E 41	SX 032 4
Mevagissey Museum	6C 40	SX 016 4
Mevagissey Quay Car Park	6C 40	SX 017 4
Mevagissey Tourist Information Centre	6C 40	SX 014 4
Mevagissey, Town Car Park	5C 40	SX 012 4
Middle Point	4E 33	SW 825 3
Mill Bay	4C 8	SW 354 2
Millbrook	2D 55	SX 423 5
Millbrook Lake	2E 55	SX 435 5
Millbrook, West Street Car Park	3D 55	SX 422 5
Millendreath	2F 49	SX 268 5
Millendreath Car Park	2F 49	SX 268 5
Millpool	1D 17	SW 572 3
Minack Point	6F 9	SW 387 2
Minack Theatre	5F 9	SW 387 2
Mixtow	2D 45	SX 129 5
Mixtow Pill	3E 45	SX 131 52
Mên-aver Point	5E 29	SW 792 2
Mên-y-grib Point	4B 20	SW 662 1
Mongleath	4B 30	SW 790 3
Monkey Sanctuary	4B 50	SX 284 5
Mount Batten	4E 57	SX 488 5
Mount Batten Ferry	4E 57	SX 485 5
Mount Edgcumbe, Barrow Car Park		
	5B 56	SX 450 5
Mount Edgcumbe Country Park	5B 56	SX 451 5
Mount Edgcumbe House	5B 56	SX 452 5
Mount Edgcumbe, Maker Car Park	5A 56	SX 447 5
Mount Gould	2F 57	SX 494 5
Mount Hermon	2B 22	SW 699 1
Mount's Bay	6F 15	SW 530 2
Mount Wise	3B 56	SX 457 5
Mousehole	2B 12	SW 469 2
Mousehole, The	3B 12	SW 469 2
Mousehole Beach Car Park	2C 12	SW 471 2
Mullion	4C 20	SW 678 1
Mullion Cliff	6B 20	SW 667 1
Mullion Cove	6B 20	SW 668 1
Mullion Cove Car Park	5C 20	SW 670 1
Mullion Cove Hotel Car Park	6B 20	SW 666 1
Mullion Island	6A 20	SW 659 1
Mullion Village Car Park	4C 20	SW 678 1
Mutley	2E 57	SX 483 55
Mutton Cove	4B 56	SX 452 53
Mylor Churchtown	1E 31	SW 820 35
Mylor Churchtown Car Park	1E 31	SW 820 35
Mylor Yacht Harbour Car Park	1E 31	SW 820 3

re Cove	1D **27**	SW 798 240
re Head	5F **35**	SW 915 369
	6F **29**	SW 800 246
re Head Car Park	6A **36**	SW 921 379
re Point	5F **29**	SW 800 251
rkurs	3F **51**	SX 322 558
rkurs Cross	2F **51**	SX 321 560
rrows, The	4B **56**	SX 457 533
tional Marine Aquarium	3E **57**	SX 485 540
tional Maritime Museum Cornwall	4D **31**	SW 813 324
aland Point	5E **47**	SX 190 502
lly's Cove	2D **27**	SW 797 234
wlyn	6E **13**	SW 462 286
wporth Head	6B **30**	SW 798 300
Man's Land	2A **50**	SX 275 566
rth-hill Point	3B **32**	SW 859 333
o-dour Cove	3E **21**	SW 667 157
d Guildhall Museum & Gaol	3E **49**	SX 255 532
ter Broady Cove	6F **55**	SX 442 489
byer Point	2E **39**	SX 024 426
ace Cove	4B **46**	SX 162 511
lmer Point	5A **56**	SX 440 526
r	2E **43**	SX 076 535
r Beach	2F **43**	SX 082 532
Beach Car Park	2F **43**	SX 086 532
Beach Nature Reserve	2F **43**	SX 082 532
rbean Cove	6E **29**	SW 796 249
rc-an-als-Cliff	4D **19**	SW 633 249
rc Bean Cove	3E **21**	SW 667 158
	6F **19**	SW 654 220
rc Caragloose Cove	5A **36**	SW 929 384
rc Trammel Cove	2B **18**	SW 619 262
r Harbour (Imerys) Car Park	3E **43**	SX 073 528
rkers Cross	3C **48**	SX 231 530
rn Voose Cove	4D **23**	SW 714 130
r Sands	3F **43**	SX 083 528
rson's Beach	4D **29**	SW 786 269
rson's Cove	4B **46**	SX 167 511
r Station	1E **43**	SX 077 541
ssage Cove	4B **28**	SW 764 268
ul	1B **12**	SW 464 270
ynter's Cove	4D **11**	SW 427 230
dngwinian	3A **20**	SW 651 209
dn-mên-an-mere	6F **9**	SW 384 216
dnvadan	6C **34**	SW 882 359
lltras Point	5D **9**	SW 361 221
n-a-maen	3D **39**	SX 017 411
nare	4C **38**	SX 000 403
nare (Dodman Point) Car Park	4B **38**	SW 999 404
nare Point	5D **41**	SX 021 458
narrow Point	2E **31**	SW 826 348
narvon Cove	4A **28**	SW 756 263
nberth	5B **10**	SW 401 229
nberth Cove	5B **10**	SW 403 225
ncarrow Head	5A **46**	SX 151 503
ncarrow Head Car Park	4F **45**	SX 149 513
ncra Head	3E **27**	SW 809 224
ndennis Castle	5E **31**	SW 824 318
ndennis Point	5E **31**	SW 826 314
ndower Beach	3E **35**	SW 901 381
ndower Beach Car Park	3D **35**	SW 897 382
ndower Car Park	3D **35**	SW 895 380
ndower Coves	5C **8**	SW 358 229
nhallick	3D **25**	SW 765 186
njerrick Garden	6A **30**	SW 779 307
nlee Battery Car Park	5E **55**	SX 437 491
nlee Battery Nature Reserve	5F **55**	SX 440 490
nlee Cove	6F **55**	SX 442 488
nlee House Gallery & Museum	4F **13**	SW 470 300
nlee	2C **12**	SW 473 268
	6F **55**	SX 442 487
nmere Station	4B **30**	SW 798 323
nnance Point	6C **30**	SW 804 305
nnarin Point	4F **35**	SW 913 376
en Olver	6D **23**	SW 712 117
npoll	1F **45**	SX 145 545
npoll Creek	1E **45**	SX 134 542
nrose (Loe Pool West) Car Park	3D **19**	SW 638 258
nryn	2A **30**	SW 784 344
nryn Harbour Car Park	2A **30**	SW 789 342
nryn, Permarin Road Car Park	2A **30**	SW 784 345
nryn Station	2A **30**	SW 779 346
nslake Cove	5D **47**	SX 184 503
Pentewan	3C **40**	SX 019 472
Pentewan Beach	4D **41**	SX 020 469
Pentewan, West End Car Park	3C **40**	SX 017 472
Pentreath Beach	5B **22**	SW 692 127
Penventinue Cove	5C **44**	SX 117 508
Penzance	4F **13**	SW 473 302
Penzance, Harbour Car Park	4F **13**	SW 476 304
Penzance Station	4F **13**	SW 475 306
Penzance Tourist Information Centre	4F **13**	SW 476 305
Penzance Youth Hostel	4D **13**	SW 457 302
Penzer Point	4B **12**	SW 466 249
Perbargus Beach	3D **37**	SW 955 409
Perbargus Point	2D **37**	SW 957 410
Perbean Beach	2E **37**	SW 965 411
Percella Point	5F **9**	SW 388 222
Percuil	2B **32**	SW 858 340
Percuil Car Park	2B **32**	SW 858 340
Percuil River	2B **32**	SW 859 343
Perprean Cove	4F **25**	SW 783 179
Perran Downs	1B **16**	SW 553 305
Perran Sands	5F **15**	SW 539 292
Perranuthnoe	5F **15**	SW 537 295
Perranuthnoe Car Park	5F **15**	SW 539 292
Perveor Point	5C **38**	SX 005 399
Philleigh	2B **34**	SW 871 393
Phoebe's Point	6A **42**	SX 032 498
Picklecombe Point	6B **56**	SX 456 514
Pier Cove	5F **55**	SX 440 495
Pigeon Ogo	4F **21**	SW 673 142
Pipers Standing Stones, The	3E **11**	SW 434 247
Piskies Cove	4B **16**	SW 553 277
Place Ferry	4B **32**	SW 851 327
Plaidy	3F **49**	SX 262 538
Plaidy Beach	3F **49**	SX 265 538
Plain-an-Gwarry	3F **15**	SW 534 314
Plymouth	3D **57**	SX 477 543
Plymouth, Blagdon's Meadow Car Park	3F **57**	SX 501 549
Plymouth City Museum & Art Gallery	3E **57**	SX 481 549
Plymouth, Devil's Point Car Park	4C **56**	SX 461 534
Plymouth, Milehouse Park & Ride	1D **57**	SX 471 566
Plymouth, Mountbatten Car Park	4E **57**	SX 485 533
Plymouth, Mutton Cove Car Park	3B **56**	SX 452 540
Plymouth, Queen Anne's Battery Car Park	4E **57**	SX 487 538
Plymouth RC Cathedral	3D **57**	SX 471 548
Plymouth Station	2D **57**	SX 476 553
Plymouth Tourist Information Centre	4E **57**	SX 483 539
Point Spaniard	3B **12**	SW 468 255
Polbathic	1B **52**	SX 347 569
Polbream Cove	6C **22**	SW 702 114
Polbream Point	2E **23**	SW 729 158
	5B **20**	SW 666 188
Pol Cornick	3E **21**	SW 668 154
Polcries	6E **27**	SW 803 199
Poldhu Cove	4B **20**	SW 664 198
Poldhu Cove Car Park	4B **20**	SW 667 199
Poldhu Point	4B **20**	SW 662 196
Polgigga	4E **9**	SW 376 237
Polgwidden	4D **23**	SW 717 136
Polgwidden Cove	4B **28**	SW 768 269
Polhawn Cove	5D **55**	SX 420 492
Polkerris	3A **44**	SX 093 521
Polkerris Car Park	3A **44**	SX 094 523
Polkirt Beach	6C **40**	SX 016 442
Polmear	2F **43**	SX 087 535
Polnare Cove	6F **29**	SW 800 249
Polostoc Zawn	6D **9**	SW 368 214
Polpeor Cove	6C **22**	SW 699 115
Polperro	5F **47**	SX 207 509
Polperro Heritage Museum of Smuggling & Fishing	5F **47**	SX 209 509
Polperro Model Village	4F **47**	SX 206 510
Polridmouth	5B **44**	SX 103 503
Polruan	5D **45**	SX 126 508
Polruan, St Saviour's Car Park	5D **45**	SX 125 508
Polruan to Fowey Ferry	4D **45**	SX 125 513
Polruan, Wellake Car Park	5E **45**	SX 131 506
Polruddan Cove	3D **41**	SX 025 474
Poltesco	2E **23**	SW 724 157
Polurrian Cove	5B **20**	SW 668 187
Polvarth Point	4B **32**	SW 853 328
Poly, The	4C **30**	SW 809 327
Ponsence Cove	4C **28**	SW 777 261
Ponsongath	4C **24**	SW 755 179
Pont	3F **45**	SX 143 524
Pont Pill	4E **45**	SX 133 515

Place	Ref	Grid
Pordenack Point	3B **8**	SW 345 241
Porthallow	5B **48**	SX 225 519
Porthallow Cove	2D **27**	SW 797 232
Porthallow Cove Car Park	2D **27**	SW 797 231
Porthbean Beach	5C **34**	SW 883 367
Porthbeer Cove	4F **25**	SW 783 173
Porthbeor Beach	5C **32**	SW 862 319
Porth Chapel	6F **9**	SW 381 218
Porthcurnick Beach	6B **34**	SW 879 359
Porth Curno	5F **9**	SW 387 222
Porthcurno	5F **9**	SW 382 227
Porthcurno Car Park	5F **9**	SW 384 225
Porthcurno Telegraph Museum	5F **9**	SW 384 226
Porth Farm (Towan Beach) Car Park	4C **32**	SW 867 328
Porthguarnon	5C **10**	SW 410 229
Porthgwarra	6E **9**	SW 371 218
Porthgwarra Car Park	6E **9**	SW 371 217
Porthhallow	2D **27**	SW 796 231
Porthkerris Car Park	3E **27**	SW 806 227
Porthkerris Cove	3E **27**	SW 806 227
Porthleven	3C **18**	SW 629 259
Porthleven, Highburrow Car Park	3D **19**	SW 634 252
Porthleven, Kittos Field Car Park	3C **18**	SW 628 259
Porthleven Sands	4E **19**	SW 641 241
Porthleven, Shrubberies Hill Car Park	3D **19**	SW 631 255
Porth Loe	6D **9**	SW 364 219
Porthluney Beach / Caerhays Car Park	2F **37**	SW 974 413
Porthluney Cove	2F **37**	SW 973 411
Porthmellin Head	4C **32**	SW 868 320
Porth Navas	3A **28**	SW 751 278
Portholland Car Park	2D **37**	SW 959 412
Porthoustock	4E **27**	SW 805 218
Porthoustock Beach Car Park	4E **27**	SW 807 218
Porthoustock Point	4F **27**	SW 810 216
Porthpean Car Park	5A **42**	SX 030 506
Portloe	4B **36**	SW 937 394
Portloe Car Park	4B **36**	SW 938 396
Portloe Point	4C **36**	SW 940 393
Portlooe	4D **49**	SX 241 527
Portmellon	1D **39**	SX 015 438
Portmellon Cove	1D **39**	SX 016 439
Portnadler Bay	5D **49**	SX 247 513
Portscatho	1D **33**	SW 876 352
Portscatho Car Park	6B **34**	SW 876 357
Portwrinkle	4C **52**	SX 355 538
Portwrinkle Car Park	4C **52**	SX 357 538
Pound, The	5F **21**	SW 673 136
Praa Sands	3E **17**	SW 580 281
Praa Sands (1) Car Park	3D **17**	SW 577 281
Praa Sands (2) Car Park	3D **17**	SW 579 280
Predannack Head	2E **21**	SW 660 162
Predannack Wollas Car Park	2E **21**	SW 668 162
Prilla Cove	5D **23**	SW 717 124
Prisk Cove	3E **29**	SW 795 277
Prussia Cove	3B **16**	SW 555 282
Prussia Cove Car Park	3B **16**	SW 555 281
Queener Point	6C **54**	SX 415 489
Rame	5D **55**	SX 425 493
Rame Head	6D **55**	SX 420 482
Rame Head Car Park	6D **55**	SX 421 487
Ravenness Point	5B **56**	SX 459 524
Raven's Cliff, The	5B **56**	SX 459 524
Readymoney	4C **44**	SX 117 510
Redding Point	6B **56**	SX 459 518
Rescassa	2A **38**	SW 982 424
Rill Point	5F **21**	SW 673 135
Rinsey	4F **17**	SW 593 272
Rinsey Car Park	4F **17**	SW 591 271
Rinsey Head	5E **17**	SW 589 269
Rinsey West Cliff	4E **17**	SW 588 272
River Fowey	2D **45**	SX 125 532
River Seaton	2D **51**	SX 304 569
Ropehaven	2E **41**	SX 035 489
Ropehaven Cliffs Nature Reserve	1E **41**	SX 033 491
Ropehaven Cliffs Nature Reserve Car Park	2E **41**	SX 033 489
Rosemodress Cliff	4F **11**	SW 445 234
Rosemullion Head	3E **29**	SW 797 279
Rosenithon	4E **27**	SW 801 212
Rosevine	5B **34**	SW 879 363
Roskilly's Organic Farm	5D **27**	SW 793 206
Roskorwell	2D **27**	SW 794 238
Roskruge Beacon	2B **26**	SW 779 231
Rosudgeon	2B **16**	SW 556 295
Rosudgeon Common	2B **16**	SW 556 295
Rôskestal West Cliff	5D **9**	SW 363 242
Ruan High Lanes	2E **35**	SW 902 395
Ruan Major	1C **22**	SW 703 163
Ruan Minor	2E **23**	SW 720 151
Ruan Minor Car Park	2D **23**	SW 719 151
Ruan Pool	2B **22**	SW 696 155
St Anthony	4B **32**	SW 856 322
St Anthony Head	5A **32**	SW 846 314
St Anthony Head Car Park	5A **32**	SW 848 317
St Anthony-in-Meneage	5D **29**	SW 783 248
St Anthony-in-Meneage Car Park	5D **29**	SW 782 248
St Austell Bay	5D **43**	SX 062 506
St Blazey	1D **43**	SX 068 546
St Blazey Gate	2D **43**	SX 060 537
St Buryan	2B **10**	SW 409 257
St Catherine's Castle	5C **44**	SX 114 510
St Catherine's Point	5C **44**	SX 118 509
St Clement's Isle	2C **12**	SW 474 264
St George's Island	5E **49**	SX 257 514
St Gluvias	2A **30**	SW 782 347
St John	1B **54**	SX 409 533
St Just in Roseland	1B **32**	SW 852 355
St Just in Roseland Car Park	1A **32**	SW 849 357
St Just Pool	1A **32**	SW 842 355
St Keverne	4D **27**	SW 790 213
St Keverne Beacon Car Park	2E **25**	SW 772 198
St Levan	5F **9**	SW 380 221
St Levan Church Car Park	5F **9**	SW 380 223
St Loy's Cove	4D **11**	SW 423 232
St Martin	1F **49**	SX 261 554
St Mawes	3A **32**	SW 847 331
St Mawes Car Park	3A **32**	SW 847 331
St Mawes Castle	4A **32**	SW 841 327
St Mawes Ferry	4E **31**	SW 828 325
St Mawes Harbour	4A **32**	SW 847 324
St Mawes Tourist Information Centre	3A **32**	SW 848 331
St Michael Caerhays	1E **37**	SW 963 424
St Michael's Mount	5D **15**	SW 514 298
St Ruan	2D **23**	SW 716 155
Samphire Beach	5D **49**	SX 248 511
Sandheap Point	4B **46**	SX 163 513
Sandway Point	4F **55**	SX 441 500
Sandy Cove	6A **44**	SX 099 494
Sango Point	1E **55**	SX 431 533
Sconhoe Beach	4C **40**	SX 018 461
Seaton	4D **51**	SX 302 545
Seaton Beach	4D **51**	SX 302 544
Seaton (Cornwall), Seaton Beach Car Park	4D **51**	SX 303 544
Seaton (Cornwall), Seaton Bridge Car Park	4D **51**	SX 304 544
Seaton (Cornwall) Valley Country Park Car Park	4D **51**	SX 302 545
Seaton Valley North Nature Reserve	3D **51**	SX 303 550
Sennen	2C **8**	SW 356 254
Sennen Beach Car Park	1C **8**	SW 354 263
Sennen Cove	1C **8**	SW 354 264
Sennen Cove Harbour Car Park	1C **8**	SW 350 264
Sennen Cove Lifeboat Station	1C **8**	SW 351 264
Sennen Cove Visitor Information Point	1C **8**	SW 352 264
Shannick Point	4F **35**	SW 915 374
Sharrow Cliff	2A **54**	SX 390 521
Sharrow Grotto	2A **54**	SX 393 521
Sharrow Point	2A **54**	SX 392 521
Sheffield	2A **12**	SW 457 261
Sheviock	2D **53**	SX 369 551
Shortacross	1B **50**	SX 288 572
Shutta	3E **49**	SX 258 531
Silvermine Point	6A **42**	SX 032 490
Skerrish, The	4A **52**	SX 334 533
Skinner's Ball Cliff	4D **53**	SX 365 531
Sound, The	6D **57**	SX 474 513
Southground Cliffs	5B **44**	SX 109 500
Southground Point	5B **44**	SX 104 500
Sowden's Bridge	1C **48**	SX 230 553
Sparnon	3A **10**	SW 398 242
Spernic Cove	5C **24**	SW 752 161
Spit Point	3E **43**	SX 075 522
Stackhouse Cove	3A **16**	SW 548 281
Stoke	2C **56**	SX 464 553
Stonehouse	4C **56**	SX 463 537
Stuckumb Point	6C **40**	SX 017 446
Swan Pool	5C **30**	SW 801 315
Swanpool Beach	5C **30**	SW 802 315

vanpool Car Park	5C **30**	SW 801 312
vanpool Nature Reserve	5C **30**	SW 801 316
vanpool Point	5C **30**	SW 807 313
lland	5B **48**	SX 229 516
lland Bay	5B **48**	SX 227 511
lland Bay Car Park	5B **48**	SX 223 516
vern Beach	4A **32**	SW 844 329
ncreek	4C **48**	SX 232 525
rras Bridge	1D **49**	SX 248 555
orny Cliff	1E **23**	SW 729 161
ldhu	1E **21**	SW 660 174
ll Point	4D **29**	SW 782 267
l Toft	4F **11**	SW 444 232
rpoint	2A **56**	SX 438 552
rpoint Ferry	2A **56**	SX 444 551
wan Beach	4D **33**	SW 870 329
aboe Cross	1A **24**	SW 736 205
aboe Cross Car Park	1A **24**	SW 735 206
eal	1D **23**	SW 717 160
eath	4B **28**	SW 763 260
ebah Garden	3B **28**	SW 767 275
edavoe	6D **13**	SW 454 286
een	4A **10**	SW 394 230
een Car Park	4A **10**	SW 394 230
een Cliff	5B **10**	SW 401 223
	5A **10**	SW 392 224
efusis Point	3D **31**	SW 817 335
egantle Car Park	1A **54**	SX 390 531
egantle Cliff	5F **53**	SX 387 526
egantle Down	5F **53**	SX 389 527
egantle Ranges (Danger Area)	5E **53**	SX 377 529
egarne	3C **26**	SW 784 229
egear Point	3C **18**	SW 621 258
egiffian Burial Chamber	3E **11**	SW 430 244
egiskey	4C **40**	SX 011 463
egrehan Garden	2C **42**	SX 051 536
egrehan Mills	2B **42**	SX 045 536
egurnow Cliff	4F **11**	SW 448 236
elan	3B **24**	SW 745 188
eleaver Cliff	5E **25**	SW 771 161
elew	1D **31**	SW 812 353
elowia	2C **50**	SX 297 565
enarren	2E **41**	SX 033 486
enarth Bridge	2A **28**	SW 757 282
enewan	2C **46**	SX 174 533
enona Car Park	1F **35**	SW 911 409
enow Cove	5F **15**	SW 531 298
equean Cliff	2A **18**	SW 604 267
ereife	5D **13**	SW 452 295
escowe	1D **17**	SW 578 309
esowes Green	2F **17**	SW 594 292
ethill Cliffs	4E **53**	SX 372 534
evarrack	3F **13**	SW 479 316
Trevarrick	1A **38**	SW 982 430
Trevean Cove	3A **16**	SW 544 287
Trevedran Cliff	5C **10**	SW 415 229
Trevescan	3C **8**	SW 355 248
Trevescan Cliff	2B **8**	SW 344 252
Trevilley	3C **8**	SW 357 245
Trevilley Cliff	4B **8**	SW 349 239
Trewavas Cliff	5F **17**	SW 597 264
Trewavas Head	5F **17**	SW 595 264
Trewithian	4B **34**	SW 878 372
Treworga	1D **35**	SW 897 402
Treworlas	3D **35**	SW 892 385
Treworthal	3C **34**	SW 881 389
Tribbens, The	1B **8**	SW 348 265
Truthwall	2E **15**	SW 525 325
Turbot Point	1E **39**	SX 027 430
Turnchapel	5F **57**	SX 494 528
Tywardreath	1F **43**	SX 085 543
Tywardreath Marsh Nature Reserve	1E **43**	SX 075 542
Vault Beach	4D **39**	SX 010 407
Vellan Head	4E **21**	SW 667 149
Veryan	2F **35**	SW 915 394
Veryan Bay	4E **37**	SW 964 395
Veryan Green	2F **35**	SW 919 399
Wallace Beach	4E **49**	SX 252 521
Watch House Cove	5A **46**	SX 156 508
Watchhouse Point	2F **37**	SW 971 410
Watergate	2C **48**	SX 233 544
Western King Point	4C **56**	SX 461 532
West Looe	3E **49**	SX 253 532
West Penslake Cove	5D **47**	SX 183 504
West Portholland	2D **37**	SW 957 411
West Watergate	3A **48**	SX 212 530
Wherry Town	5E **13**	SW 467 294
Whitecross	3E **45**	SX 139 527
Whitesand Bay Car Park	1C **8**	SW 358 263
Whitsand Bay	6E **53**	SX 374 517
Widegates	1B **50**	SX 284 579
Wiggle Car Park	4C **54**	SX 418 503
Wiggle Cliff	4C **54**	SX 417 503
Wilderness Point	4B **56**	SX 456 531
Windmill Farm Nature Reserve	2B **22**	SW 691 153
Zawn Gamper	4E **11**	SW 437 230
Zawn Kellys	5C **8**	SW 359 226
Zawn Organ	4B **12**	SW 461 242
Zawn Reeth	4C **8**	SW 352 238
Zawn Trevilly	4B **8**	SW 348 239
Zawn Vinoc	5C **24**	SW 758 167
Zawn Wells	3B **8**	SW 345 243
Zoar	2C **24**	SW 759 198
Zone Point	6B **32**	SW 850 309

South West Coast Path - Route Planner
Lands End to Plymouth

Key: **i** Information Centre Hotel / B&B ▲ Youth Hostel ‖ Restaurant ☕ Cafe (Seasonal opening)
✕ Campsite (Seasonal opening) Shop Public House P Petrol Station ⋁⋁ Ferry / Wade

From Lands End

From Lands End	From Plymouth	Location	Facilities
0 km	252	**LANDS END**	🛏 ‖
6.1	245.9	**Porthgwarra**	🛒
8.1	243.9	**Porthcurno**	🛏 ✕ ‖ 🍺 ☕ 🛒
		0.5km - Treen (St Leven)	‖ 🍺
10.1	241.9	**Penberth**	✕
		1km - St Buryan	🛏 ✕ 🛒
16.8	235.2	**Lamorna**	🛏 ✕ 🍺
20.7	231.3	**Mousehole**	🛏 ‖ 🍺 ☕ 🛒
23.4	228.6	**Newlyn**	‖ 🍺 🛒
26.6	225.4	**Penzance**	**i** 🛏 ▲ ✕ ‖ 🍺 ☕ 🛒 P
31.6	220.4	**Marazion**	🛏 ✕ ‖ 🍺 ☕ 🛒
35.4	216.6	**Perranuthnoe**	‖ 🍺 ☕
		4.5km - Relubbus	✕
		0.5km - Kenneggy	✕ ‖ 🍺
41.8	210.2	**Praa Sands**	🛏 ✕ ‖ 🍺 ☕ 🛒
49	203	**Porthleven**	🛏 ✕ ‖ 🍺 ☕ 🛒
53.9	198.1	**Gunwalloe**	🛏 ✕ ‖ 🍺
56.2	195.8	**Church Cove (Gunwalloe)**	
		2.5km - Cury	🛏 ✕
57.9	192.8	**Poldhu Cove**	☕ 🛒
59.2	191.5	**Polurrian Cove**	
		1km - Mullion	🛏 ✕ ‖ 🍺 🛒
60.5	190.2	**Mullion Cove**	🛏 ✕ ☕
68.1	183.9	Kynance Cove	☕
71.6	180.4	**Lizard Point / The Lizard**	🛏 ▲ ✕ ‖ 🍺 ☕ 🛒
77.2	174.8	**Cadgwith**	🛏 ‖ 🍺 🛒
		1km - Ruan Minor	🛏 🛒
79.6	172.4	Kennack Sands	✕ ☕ 🛒
88.3	163.7	**Coverack**	🛏 ▲ ✕ ‖ 🍺 ☕ 🛒
94.2	157.8	**Porthoustock**	
		1.5km - St Keverne	🛏 ✕ ‖ ☕ 🛒
96.2	155.8	**Porthallow**	🛏 ‖ 🍺 ☕ 🛒
100.7	151.3	**Gillan**	🛏
104.2	147.8	St Anthony-in-Meneage	🛒
		1km - Manaccan	🛏 ‖ ☕ 🛒
108.5	143	**Helford**	🛏 ‖ 🍺 ☕ 🛒
108.5	143	**Helford Passage**	🛏 ‖ 🍺
112.3	139.7	**Mawnan**	
		1km - Mawnan Smith	‖ 🍺 ☕ 🛒
113.6	138.4	Rosemullion Head	
116.2	135.8	**Maenporth**	✕ ‖ ☕
		4km - Treverva	🛏

From Plymouth

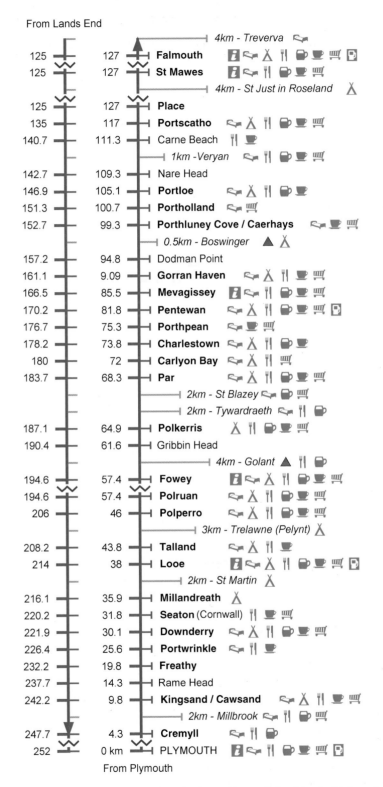

- Most campsites and caravan sites are seasonal and may not be open in the winter, check before going.
- Some caravan sites are for Caravan Club members only, check before going.
- Some cafes and beach shops are only open in summer.

Ferry Information

Ferry	From	To	Reference	Frequency
Gillan Creek	**Gillan** ∨∨	**St Anthony**	5D **29** (SW 780 253)	on demand

Operator: Antony Jenkin, Tel: 01326 231357
www.stanthony.co.uk/sailing/ferry-and-tuition.html
April 1st - October 31st, 3 hours either side of high tide
Alternatives - 1 hour walk around end of creek (recommended), or
wade 1 hour either side of low tide (not recommended).

Helford River	**Helford** ∨∨	**Helford Passage**	4B **28** (SW 761 266)	on demand

Operator: Helford Riverboats, Tel: 01326 250770
www.helford-river-boats.co.uk
Good Friday or April 1st - October 31st, 09.30 - 17.30
(09.30 - 21.30 Jun - Aug)
Alternatives - using footpath and lanes via Mawgan, Gweek & Porth
Navas (21 km / 13 miles)

Fal Estuary	**Falmouth** ∨∨	**St Mawes**	4E **31** (SW 828 328)	1 hour

Operator: Fal River Links, Tel: 01872 861910
www.falriver.co.uk/getting-about
All Year   (08.30 - 17.15)
Alternatives - 26 km / 16 miles by road (via King Harry Ferry)
Buses (88 Falmouth to Truro & 550 Truro to St Mawes)

Percuil River	**St Mawes** ∨∨	**Place**	4B **32** (SW 852 327)	30 mins.

Operator: Fal River Links, Tel: 01872 861910, www.falriver.co.uk/frl
Early April - End of October, 09.30 - 17.00
Alternatives - using footpaths and lanes (14.5 km / 9 miles)
Bus (550 St Mawes to Gerrans) and walk Gerrans to Place

River Fowey	**Fowey** ∨∨	**Polruan**	4D **45** (SX 126 513)	10-15 mins.

Operator: C Toms & Son Ltd., Tel: 01726 870232
www.ctomsandson.co.uk/polruanferry.html
All Year, 07.30 - 23.00 (07.30 - 19.00 Oct - April)
Alternatives - Bodinnick Ferry and footpaths (4 km / 2.5 miles)

River Tamar	**M. Edgcumbe** ∨∨ **Plymouth**		4B **56** (SX 457 536)	30 mins.

Operator: Cremyll Ferry, Tel: 01752 822105, www.cremyll-ferry.co.uk
All Year, 06.45 - 18.45
Alternatives - Bus 80 Cremyll to Kingsand, Millbrook or Torpoint &
81 Kingsand, Millbrook or Torpoint to Plymouth

Tourist Information Centres

Name	Address	Telephone
Falmouth	11 Market Strand, Prince of Wales Pier. TR11 3DF	01326 313394
Fowey	5 South Street, Fowey. PL23 1AR	01726 833616
Helston	Isaac House, Tyacke Road, Helston. TR13 8RR	0300 1234 100
Looe	The Guildhall, Fore Street, Looe. PL13 1AA	01503 262072
Mevagissey	St Georges Square, Mevagissey. PL26 6UB	01726 844440
Penzance	Welcome to West Cornwall Centre, Station Approach, Penzance. TR18 2NF	01736 335530
Plymouth	Island House, 9 The Barbican, Plymouth. PL1 2LS	01752 306330
St Mawes	Roseland Visitor Centre, The Square. TR2 5AG	01326 270440

Safety & Security when walking

GENERAL

◆ Make sure you are wearing appropriate clothing and footwear, with suitable extra clothing in case the weather changes, or if you get delayed or misjudge how long it will take you to complete the walk.
◆ Be careful, if you are inexperienced, not to undertake a walk that is too ambitious.
◆ Take plenty to eat and drink, there are not always opportunities to buy extra provisions.
◆ Be sure someone knows where you are going and when to expect you back. Let them know when you have returned as well.
◆ Although taking a mobile phone is a good idea, in some remote areas there may not be a signal and therefore should not be relied upon.
◆ When walking on roads follow the advice in the Highway Code.
◆ Always use a pavement and safe crossing points whenever possible.
◆ Where there is no pavement it is better to walk on the right hand side of the road, facing oncoming traffic.
◆ Only cross railway lines at designated places and never walk along railway lines.
◆ Good navigational skills and a compass are essential.
◆ Always take warm and waterproof clothing; conditions at coastal locations can always change quickly, even in summer.
◆ Walking boots should always be worn.
◆ Gloves and headgear are advisable too in cold weather.
◆ Other essentials to take are; a waterproof backpack, "high energy" foods, a whistle, a torch (with spare batteries and bulb), a watch, a first aid kit, water purification tablets and a survival bag.
◆ Ready made first aid kits are available with all necessary items included.
◆ High factor sunscreen should be used in sunny weather, the sun can be particularly strong and can be hidden by sea breezes. Sunglasses are advisable too.
◆ Informal paths leading to beaches can be dangerous and are best avoided.
◆ When crossing a beach, make sure you know the tide times to avoid being cut off.
◆ Some cliffs overhang or are unstable and this are not always obvious.
◆ On the coast, mist, fog and high winds are more likely and can be hazardous.

The international distress signal is six blasts of a whistle repeated at one minute intervals (the reply is three) or six flashes of light at one minute intervals (again the reply is three). In an emergency dial 999, or 112 and ask for the coastguard.

DANGER AREA - Page 53. Tregantle Ranges (with Antony Training Area).
When the Ranges to the south of Tregantle Fort are not being used for live firing, the MOD owned beach is open for public use.
The SW Coastal Path runs through the Training Area alongside the B3247 so that access is not interrupted by the use of the Firing Ranges.

For further information on live firing times, contact 01752 822516.

THE COUNTRY CODE

◆ Be safe - plan ahead and follow any signs.
Even when going out locally, it's best to get the latest information about where and when you can go; for example, your rights to go onto some areas of open land may be restricted while work is carried out, for safety reasons or during breeding seasons. Follow advice and local signs, and be prepared for the unexpected.
◆ Leave gates and property as you find them.
Please respect the working life of the countryside, as our actions can affect people's livelihoods, our heritage, and the safety and welfare of animals and ourselves.
◆ Protect plants and animals, and take your litter home.
We have a responsibility to protect our countryside now and for future generations, so make sure you don't harm animals, birds, plants, or trees. Fires can be as devastating to wildlife and habitats as they are to people and property.
◆ Keep dogs under close control.
The countryside is a great place to exercise dogs, but it's every owner's duty to make sure their dog is not a danger or nuisance to farm animals, wildlife or other people.
◆ Consider other people.
Showing consideration and respect for other people makes the countryside a pleasant environment for everyone - at home, at work and at leisure.

QR codes Scan for the latest information using your mobile device

Useful Information

 Tide Times

Information on Tide Times
www.tidetimes.org.uk
includes sunrise and sunset times

Weather

Met Office
www.metoffice.gov.uk

 Countryside Access

For more information visit
www.countrysideaccess.gov.uk

OS Map Reading

OS Map reading made easy

 OS National Grid

OS Using the National Grid

Danger Areas

Ministry of Defence Safety and Access
www.access.mod.uk

 Traveline South West

SW Public Transport Information
www.travelinesw.com
Getting from A to B by public transport

UKcampsite

Comprehensive campsite directory
for campers and caravanners
www.ukcampsite.co.uk